Of

All

The

Corners

To

Forget

Gian Lombardo

M E B

Acknowledgment is made to the magazines where some
of the work has previously appeared: "Concentric Circles,"
www.canwehaveourballback.com; "Calling All Pageturners," "Field of
View" & "Head in the Stars," *Dirigible;* "On the Mark" & "Indefinite
Article," *Double Room;* "The Stuff," "Suspect Compass," "Middle
Road" & "With Fish," *The End Review;* "Partial Rhythm Primate
Laughing," *Fence;* "A Book Full of Bites" & "End of the Beginning,"
gestalten; "Finders Keepers," *Inscape;* "Fleece Wisecracks, Fortune's
Dome," "The Wonder" & "Unfinished," *Logodaedalus;* "Not Want
Get What," *www.mipoesias.com;* "Rain Calling Different Names" &
"Drowning, If By Another Name," *Pavement Saw;* "Devil of a Time,"
"Trick Under Treat," "Painting the Box" & "Appearances May Be,"
Sentence; "The Stuff," "Suspect Compass," "Middle Road" & "To
Cry For," & "Back Affronted," *www.slope.org;* "Category Left
Unfilled," "Dance to the Death of the Novel," "On Account of
Wry Numbers," "Odds, Fallen, Cracked to Bits" & "Over Easy —
Hold the Brains," *www.stridemag.com;* "Cage, Door Open" &
"Uncertain Lies About the Red Bowl," *Verse;* the complete section
"Of All the Corners to Forget," *Washington Review;* and "Short
Catalog of Faces" & "Exegesis of the Still Life," *Web del sol.*
Many thanks are given to the editors of these publications.

ISBN 0-923389-68-7

Cover Painting:
Kay Sage, *Unusual Thursday,* 1951
Oil on canvas, 32″ × 39″
New Britain Museum of American Art
Gift of Mrs. Naum Gabo 1978.90
Photo Credit: Michael Agee

Meeting Eyes Bindery
An Imprint of Spuyten Duyvil
P.O. Box 1852
Cathedral Station
New York, NY 10025
1-800-886-5304

Contents

for Margie

What

For

To The
Point

I can't tell you about it. It's what I have been telling you about. This inability to explain, describe.

Describe what I'm unable. I've experienced, I've shuddered, but who'd believe?

Believe me, I haven't said anything yet. But you say you've heard it all before. Before I could begin to tell you about it.

Painting
The Box

The differences between things are not the differences. The similarities are not similar.

What's said is not necessarily what's heard. What's heard is not always what's said.

Here, everything's close. There, everything's far away.

Little by little the corner grows smaller and the landscape beyond larger and larger. . .

Bean

It's not mentioned much in this context. Or in any other. That's a fact.

It's deficient in this text. Not to mention any other. That's sad.

It's cropped up on occasion. If the time were right, there'd be a mention somewhere.

Like a hill that once was.

Stuck
At Ones

If I have two hands (which I do), someone might try to persuade me to relinquish one. To say: Hand it over.

If I were done, someone might engage me to begin anew. To tender: That it ain't over until it's over.

Not that if I fell to pieces someone might put them back together. (There's remains all over:

To fit each piece with its complement until there's just one left.

Global
Positioning

While I was away, I was never here. Easy to miss, I guess, leaving not much of an impression, all here and there. Or nowhere.

While I was away, I was hanging around all the time. Not too easy to miss, a shadow everyone's unable to shake, lurking here and there, leaving no place safe.

While I was here, I was never away. More of a presence, no fonder did the heart grow, easily pining for the hoped-for leaving.

While I was here, I was off and about everywhere. Less of an absence, the familiarity, being easy, bred contempt and left no stone unturned.

Covering
The Basis

If you see me, then we risk the same. If we risk the same, does that mean we see eye to eye?

Questions of vision notwithstanding, let's not consider the raise and its occasionally lethal consequence: The higher the raise, the longer the fall, the longer the harder. . .

It hits you that if something's in the open, theoretically it's more easily seen than if it weren't. (Still a standing query in some last resorts.)

Much like using your noggin to know what to do with your head when it rains.

On The Mark

These days only the periods between houses can be seen. The patchwork of homes has become a net from which no one escapes.

There's only endstops rolling to no beginning. To negotiate such expanses stocked with shiny ball bearings requires rollicking legwork.

Thus, a point can always be inserted between two others. It's not a futile endeavor; on the contrary, the activity ignites a consuming insistence.

Things being equal, a nest of periods makes a hard bed in which to lie. But it's the grammar behind them that carries the burden.

Far-Sighted
Bull's Eye

Almost as if asleep. But resting on your back, eyes closed will always give that appearance.

Who nods off having too good a time? In mid-laugh, while circling the dance floor, does the coil of pleasure shuffle off?

The clutch of the all-too-probable never lets you wander out of reach. But that doesn't mean the dance is off limits.

Yet, no matter how gaily, you still drag your carcass. As much as you want, step lively, almost, but not quite on target.

Indefinite
Article

Perhaps it's the wall that begs me to pay attention to its miraculous instructions.

While it's always possible to misinterpret, there hasn't been a rash of misgivings with which to indulge.

If, by chance, nothing's been forgiven, there's no reason to rush into a garden luxuriant in forgetfulness.

Maybe that's all that needs to be followed — for what's been rendered has also been divided, with each division a tiny step on which to perch.

Back
Door

Be vengeful and multiplex. Overload cables and air-waves. Let the heavens hum.

And with such music do the spheres move? Only by the refrain least subject to slipping the mind.

Supine, everything looks up. High there, and away, and afar.

No more space within which to fall: What shame is there in that?

A Vote
Of No Return

Every room in this house is identical. This house is no
better than a cave.

Who's the man who'd be king? In this domain who'd
master the notion of place (if every room's the same)?

Calling from where?

Looks like what?

Wait a minute

                    I'll put you on hold. . .

Hard Sell,
Soft Shoe

Who throws a war no further than a kitchen sink? The measure of trust never quite on par with the measure of a smile. . .

Given an inch, I'd walk a mile. Then make up all sorts of things so ludicrous it's hard to imagine what the truth would be even if it stood up and licked you on the nose. . .

There's no shortage of names on the list. Weighed heavily to the snide, it'd have to roll over and demand to be scratched on the belly. . .

While the itch remains, nothing else matters. Just a total lack of doubt regarding the protocol: If it moves, salute. Otherwise, find out what's on the other foot. . .

Upstart

I don't understand. A simple declarative. That's easy: Understandable: The position beneath comprehension with a distinctly singular non-existent view.

From below, there, too much unlike from above, too much rock. Almost everything on which to make a stand.

Suppose this matter of perception at loggerheads. Suppose its breadth and suffer longstanding. Suppose its exclusion and turn outstanding.

Now tread lightly. Suppose any excursion and choose freestanding.

Never mind: Suppose best vantage: Beneath what's known to work — and with work even the upstanding take advantage and lie down.

Appearances
May Be

I come from somewhere. I'm going somewhere. That's my conundrum: Wherever I go I bring nothing but movement.

Yet nothing comes from me. Nothing goes. Whenever I rest, there's just stillness.

It's not nothing: Everyone comes from somewhere. Going somewhere.

It's like placing a book on a seat, then walking away, letting the train sustain its movement, letting the book lie there no matter what.

Indeterminate
Scales

Rain Calling
Different Names

It's the sound of tiny firecrackers. No flashes. No concussion. Some fuses hiss, some catch.

No telling how many sparks until the war's won. Some days there's no trace.

Category
Left Unfilled

Not in this room. Not on this life. Never in this house.
No way this is going down.

Until it's fallen over. Fall under. Thrown over. Through.

Dance To The
Death Of The Novel

It's gotten calmer. They've stopped asking light to take it off. All off. So heavy the breath. As if a tree rolled onto rib-box. Rasp of blade against bar.

Eye to keyhole notes friction. No ear for second law of thermodynamics. Knocks against wall. Nose tones grindstone, recovers and preaches conservation of matter.

So light on feet. Once the crawl. Now the swing. Gesture for romance heading out the door.

More Room
In Hunting Blind

Where bear shits. No one hears the sound of one drought falling. Until thunder clap.

Then, all claws scratching at seams of earth until they bleed. Time to walk under stars. Lasts a night as long as drink without breath. As long as days are drunk. Stagger among clouds. And next time? Howl, dogs, only to furnish face to tomorrow.

Where it left off, deaf in forest, one hand striking another. If any remains, fire stops at trough.

Drowning,
If By Another Name

Were as swept as continually rising. Mouth ready. Arms
slash. Whereas gone under how many times? Where's
the trick? When disappear?

In one inch. One second. Stuffed into mirror over head.
A magnet as sweet as wet.

What's understood what surface draws.

On Account
Of Wry Numbers

Click, no hum. A dead line along the dress, where sequence could not be found. But rather fond of fabric. Approach as curtains in wind. Always wind.

Less on downdraft, the upturn. Syncope on menu. One less, two less. Fingers drum. Where dinner could be. Better flounder than famine.

Long dress where skin. No connection without ground. Answer as wind this lying.

Odds, Fallen,
Cracked To Bits

Not enough spilled. What cannot be put in order. Always crying at the unwrapped end. Who makes who doesn't.

Sick of one thing and another. Take up body from inside out. When on the outside show. Be proud of tremor tearing strata nowhere safe to walk.

Not Want
Get What

Brushed across forehead. Minor reprieve from asking. Wish list: Rain after drought, doughnuts before confession, sprinkle of rumor slightly on rabbit's ears. All in reception.

Far from gestation, moved by another locale. Gather strangers here. Welcome market commodity. By the barrel. Grass by any other song as sweet as hair on fire.

Not in the back nor in the wrist a manner holds sway. One two three no four inclement dance. First accent then beware of gift without mouth.

More
Or Less

The straw for a camel, or the shoe's want of a nail —
either way the undertaking sinks.

Always the struggle for the insufferable, impossible
equilibrium of *le mot juste,* the when.

That, and the question of which wreaks less havoc:
Undershooting or overshooting the mark?

A Book
Full Of Bites

Patient above. Some swell, fine while rocked. Seek cure for hooks skating crossing line. Time to stand up in arms.

Below to surf ache. So much pining writhing uncontained in hand. So much ripening across pages. Daily fruit for bait swallowed to sinker on the rise.

Sides unsquared. Chance left for blind.

Doctored spline forgets sign. Enter tunnel, toll on eye, follow thin string to light. Passing for echo. Not this day but another plight. Not this breath but eclipsed sounding.

Get what gets away.

Partial Rhythm
Primate Laughing

Too soon drunk from mixed species. In this parasol no one gets out dead. Except for the passion. Wrung through and weepy. Shame on table pretending an animal belly up waiting.

Speaking under influence of whatever the monkey sees does not seem true but just another corollary to arrest.

In this howl who calls?

Turning round on way up monkey takes a back.

Over Easy—
Hold The Brains

Baked and irreparable. Downing nips of some coolant over coat and butter. But not without scenting seized.

Localized here to nub strewn. You still rake?

Of all the friends in the world to eat, mind to ingest. Put an egg on it and call it even less what used to make a ruckus on the half-shell.

Let go this date and aged purse no wicked wind pursues and for which the tongue transpires.

Fleece Wisecracks,
Fortune's Dome

Neglected fix bored on shrunken bed. Genuine flexion to oblate solid. Silk against human kindness almost another walked plank.

Count enemies trussed to sticks. Bridge cross twain, upset cart and dislodge spill nearly cried against shark scar.

Nails, nails everywhere. Nary rust nor blink.

Foot over head, head over belly, belly over board. Whip be gone. Ship breed calm.

With leg trussed over head who hides key to organism's amity? The drink, what else?

Fingers for toes shoe fits any way. No matter the gills: Hand-swat these flies then sigh.

The Wonder

A fortnight of candles lit on the table. If one is removed, of course, there'd be thirteen left. Two gone would make a dozen. Four gone leaves one for each finger, or each toe.

(Though if six were added, no digit would be ignored.)

Such an easy lesson, give or take one or a few. If there were none, there's just some mumbled curse.

And the light? Nothing quite like shadows ape drafts against walls.

Unfinished

For all intents and purposes, done even if every thread dangles. Here, a corner is missing, or a tear lacking.

Why, or wherein, the anguish? Hidden or flat on the table — some indecipherable and incurable still life — where if others were seated (remotely distinguishable in the chiaroscuro), they might drink to the death of pain.

Or one or two might linger, imply a thirst, seek absolution, a tryst or acknowledgment that having each thread unwoven prove sufficient attire.

To Cry
For

And another year's trashed. Into a bouquet of compounded stupidities.

What mends what's never kissed what comes, relinquished to the brief release of no grief.

Double
Take

Uncertain Lies
About The Red Bowl

Inverted, it can no longer capture prayers for the dead. Instead, the dead gently tap against its walls, listening to echoes.

The cat tried to drink milk from it but someone pulled it away.

When it was made, three initials were scribed on the bottom. It also spelled a simple word, one accustomed to sun and soil.

I've put it on my head to fend off blows of unripe bananas.

Several squadrons of ants have scouted rim to base. Are they pretending to bite into the glaze, or is there really something there?

Not too long ago a fish, some sand, algae and water filled its hollow. Across the top a small paper boat floated trying to force a round world.

Struck, upside down, palm covering apex, clomp against the table. Rapidly, then slowly, then gone.

The last thing heard: the sound of a liquid, pouring from its lips, down a chest, enveloping the floor. Just that —

Concentric
Circles

Two steps forward. Three steps back. Sounds something like instructions for a dance.

All present know it takes two. At least. Or else, there's nothing —

some minuet fabricated to look like it occupies four sides —

There could be more, but you're still reduced to answering "Yea" or "Nay." (Positive inebriation at the thought of that reduction.)

The handprints on the wall could be a ruse. Worse yet, paint flaking from the ceiling.

Only a single can have it. Once touched, the contagion passes.

Would a sneeze be a sign? Or last wishes?

Turning and turning again. Each revolution approaching but never quite entering the bull's eye.

Short Stick
In Deep Pond

Game's over. The dust has settled without victory.
There's that questioning look: Last pass?

Who'd have believed. What's passed. What's come looks
like a slow dismantling. What's put where. Put away.

From the reach. Always that. A little further beyond.

Looks like some sort of a journey. Those things packed.
The movement for something else. But while some-
thing's lighter, something else must grow heavier.

Loss might be judged by weight. The lighter-than-air
wallet, the expectation charged with so much tonnage,
it crashes through the floor.

And the debris to be swept. Chairs upended on top of
tables, as if only half of everything's overturned.

Like a glass against the wall, listening for what may
move in the next room.

Devil Of
A Time

Many, many times I've thought about arming myself against barbarians. But I couldn't decide whether a barbarian was someone I wouldn't recognize, or whether it was someone I couldn't understand.

Either way, I believe I'd end up with too many barbarians.

I believe if I need an enemy to protect myself from, it's better to have a particular enemy — one I'd know was a threat.

But if I recognized that threat, wouldn't that be something familiar? I've got the feeling I'd be contravening myself.

In that case, I'd guess I'd have to be out of sorts, being something beside myself.

Across
State Lines

"Message garbled. Repeat. Resend."

Maybe it was sunspots. A short in a dangling wire. Or a stuck key.

What went in one end. What came out the other. Any similarity to fact coincidental. Names changed to protect the innocent.

One faction of words revolted. Like spring dirt overturned, it begged for new seed.

"Grabbed mess. Dug peat. Unsinned."

Don't
Quote Me

No more patience for diacritical marks. Tripped by the unexpected phonetic step.

Exceptions make the rule. Rules, themselves, demand exceptions. Not unlike a good serve, the pronunciation's all in the lips.

Sound, or whatever staunches hunger, whatever the hunger, whatever the yen, passes that way of flesh, sometimes enough to linger. Or more. But also less.

Let's halve our meal and be dunned by it.

If wrong, amid irritation utter nonsense.

Short Catalog Of
Abandoned Faces

The usual one, the coin, set in opposing directions. Thrown, it's always either/or.

A balloon whose end has become unknotted: The long exhalation unto collapse. Pity the smooth globe reduced to wrinkles.

All the colors from red to blue to green. What passes for a prism, disentangling light.

When drawn, no paper is long enough to capture each nuance. So much is lost.

The nose crimped, crest of brow falling into water, bobbing for fruit of knowledge.

But none better than the lack of disfigurement when one dreamer responds to another equally asleep.

Back
Bite

Every sentence chases its tail. Instead of leading us on, we're led back to square one.

Or:

No sentence chases its tail. Instead of arriving at square one, we're off to who-knows-where.

And:

Every sentence and no sentence simultaneously chases its tail. We're given the run-around as we stand still.

But:

We forget: Is the sentence an animal that can chase its tail? Or are we speaking figuratively? And if we can't decide? But, of course, it's what we're led to believe when we forget.

End Of
The Beginning

What refers only to itself often gets cited for trouble.
(It's necessary and expected.)

More than anything else, living under rock. First learn-
ing to crawl, then walk.

On the outside, anything goes but it's better known that
what's on the inside counts.

In the center akin to the villain curling one or more
moustaches incessantly, a quirk or tic that translates
only into annoyance.

Such chilling chatter, such a tremor in the laughter
shaking the whole town down to its knees. . .

Exegesis Of
The Still Life

What resolute optimism: The secret of everything as evinced by the arrangement of objects.

What faces north speaks volumes. To rest in the sun is the epitome of lethargies.

To the left or right: One way or the other says so and thus, or not so, not thus — but that, this and the other. (Consider the place setting: It eats not, but permits all manner of consumption.)

Who believes the countenance set side-by-side or piled? Set cross-wise in layers or jumbles? (A face for every thing and every thing in its face.)

(No need to delineate parataxis or hypotaxis for the disposition. Focal depth, however, is key.)

Without words, anything's possible. But what happens otherwise? It could be argued any display keeps on moving, even if untouched. Whatever remains, that spark's life nonetheless.

At
A Time

First, a good story says everything. And nothing? Well, whisper one into someone's ear and suffer the consequences.

Next, one good turn deserves another. And another. Sometimes it doesn't pay to stop unless you stop to pay.

Then, goodness has nothing to do with it. And everything. Too bad sometimes it's too sweet to not to skew the halo.

Last, what turns sour comes to no good. And good for nothing. Whatever gets poured into an ear has to go somewhere.

Cage,
Door Open

Escape into sky after a brush with death. If mis-heard, then death with a brush.

Just so, to live with death wielding a brush, convincing passersby to help whitewash a picket fence.

Or, with a master's hat where the halo once shone, illuminating the tableau of a dinner with a baker's dozen of guests.

But that's too easy a row to hoe.

Or, there's the hat, once a beret, now a top upside down in a corner. There's the bold use of color. The occasional broad stroke. Wide individual lines left by the bristles dispel any idea of detail.

The scene's rural, full of bending grasses, winding streams, a sky that holds a flock of storms.

A scene just waiting for someone walking by, looking in or out, murmuring something that barely registers.

Objections

The Stuff

The long note held until sound is flesh. Once flesh, it absorbs sound until only breath is left.

Alone, this exhalation lingers a bit. It takes a drink — cinnamon and red wine — until it's time to go.

Without further delay, it embarks on the grandest of journeys.

Now there's only an absence. That, and the dream of presence, the urge of hope and melancholy to break into song.

Suspect
Compass

Living under an erratic clock. First, the epileptic spin
forward to quarter to twelve, then reversed to ten of
eight: A rush of minutes screeches to an apoplectic
stop.

This eternity lasts a moment. Strictly speaking, dynas-
ties fall and rise between tocks.

Not much of a face on this wheel: It could be just about
anyone. After a rest, those appendages mark the direc-
tion of a breeze.

Back bolstered by a tailwind, what remains but to shake
the clock's extended hand?

And go where no one else follows.

Middle
Road

Which hand? (Just think: You can't always be wrong.) Half the time it's something for you, if you can only guess.

And if you point correctly, there goes the surprise. (The continual shuffling behind the back, the new grin, the next in line of choices: It's the game, I suppose.) There it is — exposed.

Worst case you don't want it. You feel deceived by that other, the one unpicked, and let nothing drop into your hand.

But there could be a best case, now couldn't there?

Trick Under Treat

Not wanting to hear the pin drop, or the other shoe.
Light can only bear these wooden skeletons so long
before turning away, as if no more could be done.

Or the blush: Rows and rows of them sending their
naked pictures, mouthing come-ons each time there's a
breeze.

Since when does sun lack faith? Since when the aroma
of decomposition? Where it's only smoke and shatter of
glass earth.

And, ah, yes, the lucky ones whose flesh doesn't lapse
from bone.

With
Fish

A hunger that multiplies loaves. Little loaves growing, coupling with other loaves, breeding even more little loaves.

Take that knife smeared with butter. Better lick it, let the tongue curl. So many things get licked, let's not confuse them — at least, not so quickly.

Right. Take time. What's the rush? What's whet cuts deep. And the deeper, the longer the trail of bubbles from an approaching bottom. No, not now, but wait. Soon more than anticipation passes lips.

There yet?

Bent on that kiss, not of death, but of the other.

Back
Affronted

Could you imagine a trail of diamonds layered with fleece? Besides the greed, and the hankering for beauty, how vile can that road be? The root — as told — of all evil.

It's what shoots up, though, or through: All those telegrams rushing to remote regions. That clattering of "all-is-not-so-well" arriving in fingertip or toe.

A wake-up call hungover and drenched with inertia: What once moved would rather still — the unattainability of perpetual motion be damned! — and what's at rest wants to remain deep asleep.

So much easier to grasp and cultivate perpetual stillness, anchor for a wide-traveling mind.

Or synonym for wit's end.

Calling All
Pageturners

Always, too, a character stretched out on a bed, asking what we do inside our bodies. The answers, too, already there, likewise stretched out begging more questions.

For some, the traveler. Every motion an inexplicable visa to gain entry to another world of gestures.

For others, the porter. But who carries whom?

Sounds like the preamble to a novel gone bad: The indistinct shapes running to and fro, making all this activity from a question cast from a bed by a character too static to give chase.

Just waiting for those clichés all ears for what's next.

Field
Of View

To what hold the candle? In this obscure light, every shadow betrays the passing of a probable villain.

Flame flickers in the breath of nefarious laughter. Against walls vagrant penumbrae make sure the joke gets you. Never the other way round.

Once eyes foreclose on following faint shifts, piles of wax enter dreams.

No matter how many times, no matter how hard the try, the drop cannot be run back up the shaft.

As Many Jump
As Roll Over

Once in or out of clutches what makes life good what's
measured for gudgeons.

Look Out
Below

Same old joke: Ground approaches fast, ports breath elsewhere, strings a halo of stars.

Never known to be so funny so quickly unless teetering from one foot to another. In polite circles, no one titters at the portrayal of the vacillation of a soul supposed to be weightless.

In others, never an excuse for collapse, no matter how many cram into one body.

Finders
Keepers

This debate which disappears first: Foot or footprint?
Granted, no mark on stone or tile. Best keep in mind
sand or mud. Even some semblance in loose gravel.

Prints, rarely alone, most often shape a chain. Tug at it.
Listen to the rattle. Will there be something other than
a ghost at the end?

Escape foiled, what happens to the encumbrance
attached to ankle fetters? Is there a way out, compan-
ion's remnant?

Anything beyond what's been left?

Head
In The Stars

Feet where? On a soap box? One arm outstretched, the other holding anything from a book to a bottle of witch hazel and molasses.

What could that cure? Baldness? Hemorrhoids? The label says three times daily, not to be ingested orally.

Any word's good here. Even the obsolete and incredibly particular. They're all in wide currency. (Provided they're sound.)

Test them: Bite down. If they cry out, they might not be minted under letter of the law. Put them in an envelope and send them far away.

But if that envelope comes back to you marked "Postage Due," don't stamp your feet because one of them could be destined for a stair that breaks under the weight of the sky.

Of

All

The

Corners

To

Forget

Minstrel

This tree knows when ice forms on the river, it's time to dream. In the first dream, it remembers there's no need to cry over lost leaves. So much like a head of hair that's been rooted out by comb. With teeth full of flakes, wind stirs a slow song. Single notes rise and fall among the branches of this tree.

Preparation
(Make-Ready)

Subsequent dreams were laden with arms carrying flags. Rows and rows filing by, each marcher weighed down with bundles mistaken for swaddling, humming what could not be a lullaby. They slept not, but swept across the landscape line after line. Each filament with its own melody. Illuminated by music there'd still be a few that stumbled. Once fallen, they tire of watching the parade — where from the ground, they stretch, yawn and proceed, off key, to dream.

Thwart

Mummers, by all means, strode by, all painted tears and blood, some with dark hair in curls, an oblate smile, even a rare laugh. One ridiculous pair licked at tears, walking as if slaked masked mouth to masked mouth, swallowing salt. Passed by, out of season, jumping for joy, they feint and parry. All a mix of sorrow and folly, broken by a wall of drummers.

Basic
Trajectory

Percussive, the coughs, three in a row, quick, very quick. To the unattuned ear they sound like one. A lid slamming shut, but not quite catching neatly. In cupped hands pours a small stream of water until it just starts to overfill. To someone who can't decide which to address first: Thirst, or lips and face laden with grime. Barely distinguishable from this trespass, the order to expire, and which to address: Throw the discourse, or catch the cuss.

Beside
Rest

Dropped by the road, full bloom from seed of exhaustion. Not some pretty picture, this still life. Legs and arms drawn out, that body almost ready for quartering. Camp struck, no need to turn any covers. Except this earth's all rolled out, stakes arrayed in equipoise. No longer brinked to the lash, at this level nothing's battened, nothing pulled against the grain as if to pass and, by passing, to reach. But which way? How pitched this low there's yet ample room to be fallen.

Slow
Twitch

Ditch the differentia and bow like a duck. Avoid the
incoming. Presage myths on the outgoing. (As if they
were missives full of the romance of wings and the jar-
gon of dictators. As if they went belly up in the river
that flows through the novelty of wings.) Dried up and
framed by mirror-phase crescents, the only statements
dressed as barely musical surrejoinders. (As when none
are put aslumber.) And for what were they mistaken,
these aching strings of gutterals?

Around

All's pared just swift and swell. A spiral of skin not smoke coiled next to defused core. An explosion all heart, in the market for transubstance, giving little thought to the bloated doughnut rolling across the table. The matter's the ratio of revolution to crow's flight. Not every fancy runs afoul of such constancy. Never mind it cannot be resolved, like some deep-seated hunger all dressed up but going where many adduce whole and hole as some to none.

To Call
A Harbinger

Nun compared to sum. Once humble salted, then summered in mumbles. Another antiquated syndrome of overwrought magnets. Drawn to close quarters, elbow room folds luxury. Try to shave the access, turn the pilgrim away, to keep stepping lightly on the path, so plaint and harrow, memorizing symmetries immured in a bestiary replete with fables portraying creatures of habit.

And Left
If Answered

Same words spoken in the refrain. Otherwise? Listened by the idiot, ear cocked, altogether not indifferent. Mouth at ready, as always, lying at assumptions along the green cover. Nonplussed, as it were, before the crowds. Such a fragrant note militates for the abrasion. Anchor-free, ranging to and fro on the rug, each patter of steps framed in recognition but ultimately pitched unique.